Dad

SKYLER WOLF JONES

D.K. GODARD

Copyright © 2013 by Griffin Publishers, LLC

All rights reserved. This book or any portion thereof
may not be reproduced or used in any manner whatsoever
without the express written permission of the publisher
except for the use of brief quotations in a book review.
Printed in the United States of America

First Printing, 2013

ISBN 978-1490447261

Griffin Publishers, LLC
Saratoga Springs, UT 84043
www.griffinpublishers.com

DEDICATION

To our wonderful wives.

CONTENTS

ACKNOWLEDGMENTS

We'd like to thank each other. We know that sounds selfish, but just as it takes two to make a baby, it took both of us to make this book. That just got awkward.

More importantly, we'd like to thank our wives and test readers. Thank you for all the time you've put in by waiting for us to finish our work.

NOTE FROM SKYLER

Dude, (from Skyler)

First of all I am not a doctor, I am not certified, and this is not a subject that I have researched over the years to make calculated predictions on how you are supposed to feel. No, that is what women read. I am a dude. I am one of you that up until this moment was single and have been focusing primarily on myself and what is best for me. And of course, ultimately looking for that babe that would complete me and we could think about having a family. Well, I am only assuming you are either thinking about having a baby, or in the process of having a baby as this book found you. You're in luck. While the women can get into all the details about the process taking place inside them, we will discover the processes that occur for us "dudes" during this transition. I've even added illustrations because, like most dudes, we are extremely visual. However, if you find yourself just looking at the pictures you may need some assistance in making the next stages of your life work for you and your lady.

Now I write this book in hopes the ladies that we date, marry, or just sleep with, will remotely connect with the book to purchase it for you. If you are reading this opening and do not own a copy, buy it for yourself now, you will forever be grateful.

Again, let me emphasize, I am not a doctor of relationships, I am not a psychologist of love, I am a writer expressing the life changes one can expect to make as a man as you transition into being a parent. The thrilling part is you don't need a license to be a dad. But if you are carrying a loaded gun, be sure to shoot responsibly as pregnancy can occur regardless of your life situation.

There's no certification for being a Dad. But you still have to earn it.

Last disclaimer: I love my wife, but the things that are exciting and emotional to women are so different from that of men. And actually, I write this book because I do love my wife and it just helps put things in perspective to get the most of the simple truths of becoming a dad. In fact, she helped me through the rough drafts of this book! Enjoy your journey, but most importantly enjoy the subtle and not so subtle changes that occur when you lose the Dude and become the Dad!

Good Luck, Skyler

NOTE FROM DANIEL

Dude, (From Daniel)

I first met Skyler in an interview for a job on his team at his day job. After getting the job, he pulled me into this project and I was excited. We've each been married to our respective ladies for 7 years at this writing. Skyler has been a dad for 6 years to three boys, and I've been one for 3 years to two girls. It never ceases to amaze me that we can have so many different facets to our upbringing, but have similar dude to dad stories. With that and my independent publishing company, we were primed to get this rolling.

Humor. I love it. Who doesn't? Seriously, you don't? Go away, now. Skyler and I see life in the same basic principal (although he lives it better than I). With everything that happens to you, you can either get angry or laugh. So why not laugh? Skyler hired me onto his team when I was at a low point in my career. I'd been stuck at a dead end job for years and wanting to pursue writing and publishing more. While our day jobs occupy the hours from 8 to 5, we're always thinking of something new we can bring to you all from our own experience. And why not put in a bit of humor in it while we're at it? That's our style. Find the path to your destination and have fun while doing it.

I, like Skyler, am also not a doctor. But I did make that transition from dude to dad. Wait, did I say make? I should say, still making. You'll find that it is a continual process. And that's where it will get fun. We've tried to address those topics of highest priority for dudes and know you'll find something useful. Skyler and I have different styles just as much as we have similarities. We've grown up fairly differently yet have some of the same stories to share. So at times we'll use "we" in our stories and other times we'll use "I" or refer to the person directly telling the story. We're passionate about helping dudes become dads. One thing the world doesn't need more of are deadbeat dads. You can still be a man's man or a dude while being a Dad (which is better by the way). Enough introduction. We know you'll find something helpful here and enjoy your time while reading.

Now go read,

D. K.

Note: How to and How Not To use this book

Keep it simple. We've included pictures and most important (no the pictures weren't the important part) is that we've condensed this down to fit a dude's mind and/or pocket. We know, there's a lot going on in there….. Ok, maybe not that much, but don't get bogged down in details. That's why girls like those thick (that's what she said) pregnancy guides. This will be a quick read (not to be confused with premature ejacu…you get the point, you don't want to go through it too fast). We'll deliver the goods quickly (also what she said, thank you Skyler). You can read it all the way through or pick a subject at random. By making this book pocket size you can have it readily available, just don't use it as toilet paper in a crunch.

From Dude to Dad

TOPIC 1
WHAT TO EXPECT WHEN YOU'RE NEGLECTING

Perhaps you have seen or read the book *What to Expect When You're Expecting*. That book is filled with details on every aspect of becoming a parent and each stage of creating a life. Some of us dudes can't help but just want to skip ahead to the end because it is more of a fetus flip book to us. You hold one corner and flip the pages through as you watch the baby grow inside a neatly drawn woman. That is why our book is much more concise and consolidates the topics we tend to be more interested in. That said, our version could have the alternate title What to Expect When Your Neglecting.

Don't neglect your lady. Pregnancy is not a disease. Say that over out loud to have it sink in. Just because one morning you will wake up and look at your lady and she will be swollen from foot to face (don't quote us on the foot to face comment) doesn't mean it is contagious or abnormal. Our topic though is simple here. If you are neglecting her, you can expect nothing in return. Let's see how this works.

If you neglect your lady's emotions, you can expect the look (If you haven't received the look or know what we're talking about, good for you, you self-righteous asshole (Calm down, Skyler). Sorry, it means you have done really well thus far in your relationship and keep up the great work... I am sure week 2 in your relationship will change that, hahaha.

Neglect to give your lady kind comments (that's a penalty point in both the Dude and Dad department); you can expect to have blue balls in your near future. Yep, true blue is for you if neglecting niceties is what you do. More important than ever, now is a good time to show the gentlemen in you (this ups the Dad points). Throw out some words of encouragement, that she is still pretty, wait, drop the still, that might backfire, that she IS pretty. If you don't have anything nice to say though, Thumper is correct, don't say anything at all. Thumper is a rabbit by the way, not a stripper in Vegas or a verb. (And if you're not familiar with the rabbit, you will if you have a little girl. Prepare for pink, and animals, and princesses, etc. Just saying.)

Neglect your lady altogether and you have a set of issues that won't matter and this book certainly isn't your answer, but don't worry she probably won't be around to have to deal with you anyway. Maybe reference Dummies Guide to Knocking a Girl Up in One Night or Drunk or just an Outright Booty Call. This is not a good time to be selfish, yes the big game is on, yes, it's fight night, maybe you are almost at the end of an unbeatable level, but we're telling you this is not the time to neglect as women have incredible memories which different than ours.

Now is not the time to be selfish

Example, our memories are like highlight reels of great sex, fun moments or complete randomness. Ladies highlight reels play reruns of "You Should Have Done This" and "Who's the Douche Bag? You are!" Give her a reason to brag about you to her girlfriends by respecting her and not being bad mouthed by neglecting.

Daniel -I can't tell you how many times I've seen my wife just smile with that mushy lovey dovey smile when I've done something small like rub her lower back in the terminal stages of pregnancy. A little goes a long way, dude.

In the opening you heard Skyler mention you don't have to have a license to be a dad. This works in our favor and against us. Some dudes (lower class dudes) should go through a course of what it means to be a dad and respect their lady. Remember we aren't women bashing in this book, we are finding Dude solutions to the common occurrences that take place when becoming a dad. Let us restate this again in a way that it will sink in.

WE LOVE OUR LADIES. WE AREN'T BASHING THEM.

Need it clearer?

MAN UP OR WE COME GET YOU!

Our goal is to simply find Dude solutions to the common occurrences that take place when being and becoming a Dad.

TOPIC 2
BOOBS

Topic 1 is our soapbox. Not only does it set the tone for the book, but it has to be said.

And so to kick up into a higher gear, let's talk about a foreign topic to us Dudes. Boobs. Ok it is not foreign at all. Breasts are what we come into this world craving for nutrition and as soon as we have any type of thought processes related to testosterone we go back to craving. If you don't know, pregnant ladies have massive boobs. Yes, you can expect your lady to grow possibly double her size without paying a single dime on transplants.

Now calm down. Take a minute to breathe. Before you get excited about getting your lady pregnant for this reason hold on. That is a great thing, right. Yes, and no. They are great to look at, but if you haven't experienced having a child yet you will quickly realize that your once commonly fondled breasts have been put in a vault that you no longer have access too. Not just a vault, their boobs have detectors that actually warns them when you are about to make a move.

Like a psychic breast detector or nipple radar. And no, stealth cop-a-feels of low profile don't work either. Unfortunately, while they may look great, they're often a source of discomfort for your lady. Think about someone jacking an air compressor into a rather sensitive area on you and filling you up to the point of explosion. Yep, it can be like that.

Just like a pin up girl, your lady's breasts are now only for everyone to look at in their newly engorged size. There is one exception to the touch and taste rule, and that is your new born child. Your child will knowingly have privileges that you no longer get and actually give you the one eye as he or she enjoys a nice meal on a lactating boob almost to say, "Mwahahahahhaha, it's all mine." You don't believe me? Just try to touch your lady's boob while your child is breastfeeding. You have a better chance of robbing a bank and not getting caught then you do infiltrating the nipple Nazi guzzling away. That baby will attack with their ninja like clawing nails till you are forced to retreat to the other side of the room and just stare at what used to be yours. Alright so we are exaggerating this, right? You find out! And yes, baby nails somehow file down to razor sharp shanks.

Don't worry, you will get your revenge and it will be sweet, especially if you are having a boy. You will get the privilege of ingraining in him, through his youth, that he is not supposed to touch the lady parts until he is married or older. And right as you are telling him that, the image of him stealing your breasts for the year will pop back in your head, thus having you reemphasize until you are much older just to get the payback even if you don't believe in waiting till they are (sarcastically) 30. Call it instilling morals, call it having faith, but call it what it really is…revenge.

To be fair, are the ladies just being mean not letting us hold what is so rightfully ours, especially for us married men who have fully committed ourselves to one pair of boobs for the rest of our lives till death do us part? The answer is surprisingly, no! Easy, we know, we can practically hear all the "what the hell are these guy talking about". Imagine this for a moment. A beaver (not the perverted reference) is gnawing on your manhood for about 20 minutes every 3 hours. Right after the beaver is done your wife wants to come and play with you. As Dudes, our initial thought is to hell with it, fight through the pain and get some lovin', but realistically the answer 99 times out of 100 you are going to tell her no. This is the same with your lady's boobs. Our little spawns are gnawing them raw and then we expect them to allow our greedy hands to touch their breasts. Not likely.

Dudes, remember, this book is about solutions and options not a depressing love story. Dead ends never stopped us before, you just have to be creative. If you had a 4 wheel drive truck and you came to the end of the pavement on the road but there was several different off road pathways left to choose would you just stop? No, you throw it in 4 wheel drive and just be a little more cautious as you find your way through a new path. So what does this glorious analogy mean? Find a new path to the boobs.

One path: Lanolin! Buy it. Do your research on this product to be able to quote a full line of benefits to your defense if needed and then offer to rub it on those sensitive nipples to help her feel better. Now it isn't about you being a horny one track minded man, you are the "awe, how cute, you heard me say how tender they were and found something to help" sensitive man (5000 Dad points). And of course the only thing you heard out of that sentence was the word "tender". Don't stop there. Go a step further, tell her you read online or this book and it recommended taking a bath and massaging the milk ducts to help her prevent clogging milk ducts that can be extremely painful. Then, of course, finish up by rubbing the Lanolin in. Can you see the magic inside the service you just provided? You just got to cop a feel, yeah, it's different from the savage takedown we are use to, but it is a step in the right direction. Remember, create new paths.

Breasts are everything to us dudes and we know that, but when you threaten to take them away, a highly concentrated energy is intently focused on getting them back. You may want to take a break from the book at this point, especially if you don't already have any kids, and get some action. Don't worry, none of us that have kids would blame you and besides, this book will be here when you get back in an hour or two minutes depending on who you are.

We realize there are different types of us that are more butt men, legs, etc. we know, we are butt men ourselves, but let's face it, the jigglies, fun bags, milk jugs aka boobs are right up there with dogs; man's best friend.

TOPIC 3
FLOWER TO DEFLOWER

Let's talk about flowers in this chapter. If you are like Skyler, when you see flowers you think about Mother Nature. Ah, sensitive. Wrong. He thinks about Mother Nature sneaking in an overpriced way to get laid. Since when do flowers cost 40 to 50 dollars for a decent looking batch? (Daniel knows better. He knows they aren't a product of Mother Nature, but genetically engineered by women for women.)

We must say our take on flowers has changed since we have gotten older. Most men buy flowers for special occasions, or what we like to call un-special occasions. If you want to get the most bang for your buck on your flower purchases do us a favor, wait, do yourself a favor, do not buy flowers for her on the following days: Any holiday, her birthday, or any typical special occasion. It is like buying a card at Hallmark (no offense Hallmark) and not writing a personal note inside the card, letting someone you have never met capture the feelings you have for the person. It doesn't say much, and actually (Daniel scratches out what Skyler just said. That was a lady-like explanation and this book has no room for that).

Flowers on those days is just expected and says I'm desperate. Now, if not then, when? Good question. Go buy them right now and deliver them. Happy Tuesday, Friday, whatever day, it doesn't matter, just go buy them at the least expected time and have them delivered or deliver them yourself. Here is the extra part, don't let your flowers show up naked. (If you showed up naked at the door step to a dates house or your own house you probably wouldn't get a good response.) How do you dress up your flowers? With a nice simple note to let her you know you care. Need an example?

> *I saw these flowers and they reminded me of you.*
> *Everybody overlooked you until I picked you up.*
> *Hehehe. Just kidding you are beautiful.*

Not too cheesy, kind of funny, don't be surprised if you look down and your clothes are already off. Yes, women do mentally undress men too, it is not just a man thing. However, usually when they do it, you are Brad Pitt or Orlando Bloom. But honestly, do we really care?

This flower technique can be utilized for the dating scene, but it is 10,000 times more effective for a pregnant woman or anyone relatively new to being a dad. Flowers can be used in so many great occasions and when you get into the mode of purchasing them you will find creative ways to do it less expensively and have it mean so much more than a bouquet of store bought overpriced packaging. We hate to give away too many examples as we feel your own unique situations will allow you to best fit flowers into your life situations. But here are a few.

- Go to any florist and ask them if you can buy the leftover rose pedals from their store. Some places sale them in bags already others will just collect them for you. Either way they are cheap!

Use these rose petals to line a hallway or cover a bedroom or bed and write a simple note letting your lady know she should always walk on roses. I know, good stuff.

- Another one is to go to your local grocery store and find out when they start discounting or getting rid of flowers. These flowers are heavily discounted and look just as great and sends the same message, that you thought about her. And remember, write the note.

Let's sum up this section. You can get flowers on what others perceive to be special occasions, but if you want them to be really special, bring them out of the blue. We know we mentioned the undressing thing, but this goes a long way in overall household peace, a loving connection, and calming for your baby.

From Dude to Dad

TOPIC 4
CHICK FLICKS ARE BEER GOGGLES FOR WOMEN

Most of us can count on our fingers how many chick flicks and reality TV shows we have watched, and we can count on one hand how many we actually liked. These videos and shows need a new light shined on them. Ask yourself these questions.

- Are you in tune with your body and your lady's needs?

- Do you speak Shakespeare or with a foreign accent?

- Are your abs chiseled and do your biceps point to the heavens?

Ok, you get the point, most of us answer, no, no, and no. Why? Because we are human. Guess what? We are in luck! Some writing geniuses have given us the façade of having all these wonderful things and they package it in a thing called a chick flick. Yeah, that's right, through the magic of the screen we somehow, for one moment, become everything they have ever wanted.

Chick flicks are like the beer goggles for pregnant women.

It may not last long, and it might be done on a whim, but for that night, all is well and a good time is had. So next time you think you are winning a battle cause you got to watch your favorite team score, remember, you can either cheer for a team that has nothing to do with you, or make the switch for the night and root for yourself! If you happen to drink, why not create a complete moment by pounding a few and you can both have beer goggles for the night, kind of like role playing.

Need more convincing? When you're watching what you want, where is she? She's probably leaving you alone, right? Awesome! That's exactly what you wanted! (Dude +10). ERNT! WRONG! That's not what we are here for. Do you need to go back to chapter 1 again? We'll give you the visual version again for the slow learners.

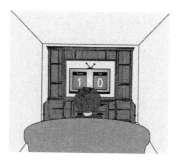

Come on! When our ladies want to watch a chick flick, where do they want you? Right smack next to her AKA, she's draped her entire pregnant self over you and making you hot and uncomfortable. So, what do you do? Turn down the air so that you don't over heat while she's snuggling. But there's another way to avoid snuggling without looking like a jerk. Offer to give her a foot rub. You get your space (you can even sneak out your phone to play a game during the movie) and you're still serving your lady. Never underestimate the power of a foot rub. The foot is connected to the leg, the leg is connected to the calf, the calf is connected to the thigh and the thighs meet right in the middle. So really. it's as easy as playing connect the dots.

TOPIC 5
WANT TO BE LAID? BE A MAID!

Have you ever felt like a god before in your relationship?
You might feel lucky, but Godlike, probably not. We found
our magical power one day and the revelation came in the
form of a bottle of all-purpose cleaner and a vacuum. We
thought since the wife was prego and tired we would clean
more than what we normally did. Skyler was amazed that he
hadn't discovered this super human power before. Can you
imagine when the wife saw him vacuuming the living room a
little star shot out of her eyes and twinkled. Like he was a
witch on a broomstick, each speckle of dust sucked into the
contraption the more powerful he grew. It was almost
euphoria or a scene from a blockbuster film. He might have
well been on a white horse riding bareback with his shirt off
riding into the distance with his long hair flowing in the wind,
wait that's Fabio.

Alright, enough analogies. If you want doors to open to magical places, pick up a dust pan, mop a floor, load a dishwasher or just do anything that feels nesty.

(Insight: women nest when they are pregnant, like cleaning, organizing, moving random shit around, etc.)

You will be equally surprised at what women notice and how little it takes when we veer slightly out of our ordinary. The more mainstream "man" you have been in the relationship the more impressed she will be. Next time she leaves the house, make a mad dash to the cleaning supplies and start scrubbing. If you're not sure where the cleaning supplies are even better and if you really didn't, check under the sinks first. Just because we picture them on all fours washing the floor in some slinky thing as they get all wet and clean to the latest house beat, that never happens. It is a crap job that they more than likely wore an oversized sweater and baggy jeans to do and the only thing glamorous about it…ya' dumbass, there isn't one. That's why you should do it. To be cautious though, clean the floor well because she might not even let you get too far if you do a good enough job and getting dirty isn't the same as feeling nasty dirty.

So what do you do if you feel you already do your "fair share" of the house hold chores? Find the ones she hates most and do those for her. Trust us on this one. We sum this idea up in the title of "Want to Get Laid? Be a Maid!"

From Dude to Dad

TOPIC 6
A SHOWER FOR EVERYONE WILLING TO COME

A baby shower sounds as exciting as…well…a baby shower. The problem with these parties is that they are advertised wrong and therefore we do not get excited about them. Let us translate the process of having a baby shower.

- Encourage your wife to invite as many friends and family to the shower, even help out with the invitations.
- Don't worry about whether the people can attend or not, this is about including everyone in this great moment.
- Your enthusiasm for wanting everyone to come and helping out will be welcomed

But here's the great part, now don't judge us for being shallow, (we're dudes so why would you) the best part is each one of those guests is going to be bringing you a present. More importantly presents that you would have to purchase if they don't bring the items. So think about this for a moment, this is your golden opportunity to save some big bucks. For those of you who got married before getting pregnant, you are probably already familiar with this concept. Remember all the free swag from the reception? Wait, you're a dude, you probably had one thing on your mind at the reception. But all that stuff in your house/apartment/hovel your first week of marriage didn't just magically appear. Your guests brought that for you. So milk the baby shower for all it's worth. (No, that's not supposed to be an innuendo for something else.)

It may cost you a few bucks in the hosting of the party, but the return on investment in buying stuff that is hard to shell out cash for will be so worth it. Have you priced diapers lately? Do you even know what a Boppi is? How about the cost of Butt Paste? Yes, there is a product that is Butt Paste and no, it's not some great prank device. Although that would be hilarious.

To sum up this great event, the more guests, the more you save. The more you participate, the more she will love you, or being hormonal and all she will be able to tolerate you, which some nights you will be satisfied with that status. Enjoy the party. Oh, before we get too sidetracked, these parties don't happen on your second child, so you are just going to have to trust us on this one and jump in head first. The only exception is if your second child is the opposite gender of the first. But it still won't be to the same degree.

There are modern versions of this party and couples are invited, don't get conned into this set up, the benefits are not structured right. Why? Your couple friends will hate you because you just signed the dudes up for torture. Your dude friends just like you don't want to bust out the pocket book to buy you that type of gift and to cap it off come and talk baby talk for a night. Plus if you have to attend you aren't capitalizing while you don't have any other kids right now, so technically you just earned yourself a free night off. It might be your last one in a long time. Not that it is a bad thing, but not even a Mastercard commercial can tell you how priceless that is. The real key in this is to come off natural and willing to help make this great party with HER family and friends be memorable. And why would she want to leave anyone out of this tremendous life changing event that is happening?

TOPIC 7
THE DEMON SEMEN

To think this whole section is about your demon semen that possessed your lady. This section is going to be very short. Do not deviate from the plan. To quickly illustrate our point go and find a child under the age of 1. Try to hold a conversation and get any point across. It won't work, ever, ever, ever, ever. Did we say ever? You will know when you are in this situation really quick and you will never make the mistake of doing it again once you have identified it. What are we talking about? A possessed pregnant lady who has taken over your normally sweet loving significant other. There will be days and nights where there is no explanation for the emotions that are channeled through your subject, it is best to do one of three things in this situation.

1. Sit there with the most intent ears you have ever put on in your life and diligently seek to understand, this type of listening is just that, listening, don't respond you will only levitate your own feet and one will be in your mouth and the other will be kicking your own ass.

2. Offer to let her be by herself or if she would like a warm bath or any food. This silently excuses you from further damage or having to be damage control

3. Call an exorcist and hope you are still alive when they arrive.

You'll never be safe with using the same method each time. Nor will there be times when only one method is sufficient. But we don't think we can emphasize enough, DO NOT ARGUE! Have you ever heard about the stories of dudes that tried to argue…Of course not! They're dead. Ok, so they aren't dead, however, women sometimes will not let things go and hold you accountable forever, this is that scenario, tread lightly. You cannot win.

You hear about win-win situations all the time, or my favorite the win-win-win situation. Well like a bastard red headed step child this is one of those pushed aside situations that you are looking for a tie-tie, or will even settle for a loss-win. Surviving to compete again will do you just fine. If Darwin's theory stood correct, your extinction rate on these occasions would become threatened. This is not to scare you, it is to absolutely frighten the ever living bejesus out of you. In fact if you have a highlighter pen, maybe just soak this whole damn section in dripping yellow. Let us just paraphrase that if you recognize your lady is completely not being herself, DO NOT ARGUE.

Alright, we're done here, moving on.

TOPIC 8
NAILING AND POUNDING

You may have a house that will allow you to make the nursery its own room, it could be part of your bedroom, it might be part of another bedroom or even a living room (FYI- a nursery is where your newborn child will spend most of its time being changed, sleeping, etc.) but start identifying a spot where the title Nursery can be placed. Imagine a bird having eggs and not being able to place them in a nest. There is no protection, security, or a place to bond before the little eggs hatch and the babies fend for themselves. This is very similar to what the Nursery provides your prego lady. The more leeway you can give your mother hen the better. Towards the terminal stages of pregnancy, your lady will start exhibiting nesting traits. They'll wash baby clothes and blankets and burp cloths 50 times over in that special, gentle, baby laundry detergent. And she'll organize, reorganize, and re-sort those piles of laundry 100 times over trying to plan the very best way to prepare for little baby. Remember last topic, don't argue. It won't make much sense to you, but it does to her.

Women have a great architectural mind, however you cannot read the blueprints nor can you guess what the vision for the room actually looks like. Our best advice, offer your services for a day or set aside a few hours to help out on anything that requires reaching high, carrying heavier items to allow her to build her little nesting sanctuary. You want to get a real reaction to your helping out, throw on an old tool belt or make shift one with nothing else on and ask her if she needs any help nailing or pounding anything (if she gets the fun joke, you're golden, if not bail out and apologize for not having any other clothes on because you did your own laundry and ruined your clothes? Timing is everything. If she's not interested, just lift up the blinds, I am sure the neighbors will get a kick out of it.

We've seen nurseries that outdo the Las Vegas strip for how much crap is shoved into one section making noises, lighting up, hiding boos, ok not boos, but good hell the baby won't remember any of it.

Skyler - With my first child I really couldn't see the significance of having a "nursery" vs. a place to put the child. I must admit, now having 3 kids there is something that translates into the kids when they have a spot and in yourself when you enter their space that gives them a calming peace.

Whether you are into it or not, like the great quote from Field of Dreams "if you build it they will come", actually that has nothing to do with it because the baby is already coming so we will just start our own quote "they are already coming, build it."

Ultimately, you're only as useful as a grunt because she won't be able to do any heavy lifting and she probably shouldn't be around any paint fumes. But something interesting we've found, is that many baby beds, chairs, swings, car seats, etc. are actually remarkably easy to assemble. But in no way act like the nursery is your den/workshop/NASCAR pit stop. You aren't in charge. You won't know what she wants. And you'll be moving the heavy stuff around multiple times before she's happy. But this is an extremely important process for your lady. There's a siren in her brain that has a very sensitive trigger. It's the security siren. They have to feel secure. That's why they snuggle with us all the time and look for a dude that can provide for them physically, financially, and emotionally. Well, now that they have a parasite in their gut, they're actually creating an emotional attachment to that thing. So much so that not only are they looking for the premium nursery for their own ease, but for the comfort of that little runt.

TOPIC 9
MY NAME IS HARRY BALS

There is so much build up to choosing the right name. Do you have a family name passed on generation after generation? Is your last name common so you want to spice up the first, or vice versa? Do you like to destroy the spelling of normal names like Brian and spell it Br(1)en, you know it's only a matter of time before numbers are in names. Naming your baby is one of the coolest things to do. Be patient and make it work for both of you. Take a look at some of the baby name websites if you need ideas of what you might like to name your baby or what to avoid as the popular name changes year to year.

Here's what Skyler did:

Something my wife and I did to create different names is on one of our road trips we read every street sign to see if it fit our last name. This is your time to speak up and let it be known you have an interest in what your child will be called the rest of their life. If you are shy or like to pick your battles wisely, I recommend choosing this as one to do so. Your connection to your unborn child is strengthened through the name you choose.

Daniel's experience is this:

My wife has a short first name and long middle and last names before we got married. But she always thought it was weird that her first name is Amy with really long middle and last names. So I wasn't allowed to pick anything too short followed by something ridiculously long. Coming up with the first name of our two girls was actually something fairly easy to do. We had a little bit of a harder time doing the middle names. Not that we couldn't come up with anything. It was more whittling it down to just one. The fashion of having more than one middle name went out a while ago. But in almost every name we thought of, there was some kind of family connection.

Wherever you get it from, as long as both of you agree, there shouldn't be any problem.

Here are a couple other great tests for names.

- Can you yell their full name out when calling for them to come home or when they are in trouble?

- Do they have options to shorten it, lengthen it, go by a fun nick name and on the opposite of that can they be teased relentlessly by other kids. Skyler once knew a kid named Harry and his last name was Bals. Now of course their name was pronounced Baals, like pals, but when you see his last name on any jersey and you hear the parents call out Harry, you put two and two together, or just the two Bals together if you know what we mean.

Picking out a name should be a fun process, don't make it work. Some people find names quickly and others don't. In fact one of Skyler's brothers had a couple of names they liked and even after he was born wasn't sure which one to pick. The names of Skyler's kids ended up as follows: Griffin Wolf Jones, Falcon Sky Jones and Phoenix Kai Jones. Middle names are representing mom and dad, first names are just flat out cool names and the last name, if you're going to keep up with someone, it might as well be the Jones'.

Skyler- Here are some cool names we will provide you with for free. Well, not free since you had to buy the book. But free from effort.

Girls: Raven, Azalyea, Winter

Boys: MacGuyver, Hawk, Bryler

TOPIC 10
HORNED TOAD

If you live in a desert you can understand what living in a drought climate is all about, it means you might be thirsty, but there ain't no water. Perhaps you have attended a doctor appointment with your lady, maybe you had a sister or someone you know deliver a baby, or maybe you were the only studious little 6th grader who paid attention in your maturations class. There is still one thing that doesn't get discovered unless you poke and prod, so to speak. The obvious part of the drought comes when your lady stops being able to see her own feet, her belly button no longer exists, and her feet are closer to cankles than legs. You guessed it, you aren't getting any. This can be partially because they no longer feel attractive, partially because it is starting to get painful, and partially because why the hell should you be satisfied when they clearly are uncomfortable. This lead up is only preparing for the real drought that follows immediately after the delivery of the baby. Doctors' orders fellas, 6 weeks. Yep, 6 big weeks for you to think about. In real time it is about 4 to 5 weeks as you are tired and excited for the baby to arrive, but fear not, your manly instincts return all too quickly. We are going to assume that everyone reading this book is the faithful type, which to us, is the only way to live true to yourself and your new family so let's think about this drought situation and how you can overcome it.

What happens when you are so stoked to get a Dr. Pepper or beverage of your choice, you place your money in the vending machine, hit the button only to find out it is out of order or sold out. After a few curse words fly you quickly try to retrieve your money. Your next step is to find your options. To keep the drink analogy going since we are talking about a drought or thirst your options are to: overpay for the step child soda of your choice, go drink the free coffee or tea with the fake sugar and nasty creamer, or make the drive to a convenient store where there is a great supply of your favorite beverage, where in which you will be suckered in to buying a snack too. These choices are a lot like the ones you will have, you could find some sort of device of sort to assist you in the process, you can try your hardest to convince your lady that your pain is equal to or greater than hers right now (good luck) or simply go to an alternative.

Skyler- While none of these options are great, the point is to not let the buildup clog the pipes till they explode. I know, it becomes a mind game where you are just trying to locate the orgasm ninja to fight him off. If you haven't already you will soon with your new child read the book, If You Give a Mouse a Cookie. Anyway this book says if you give a mouse a cookie, chances are he is going to ask for a glass of milk. And it goes through a series of things that the mouse will want if you give it the cookie. Women know this about us dudes too. If you give a dude a little lovin', chances are he's going to want more. So what do they do, exactly, don't even start. You probably will never read this chapter again as it is too painful to hear about, but just know it exists and be prepared. We are not just sexual juggernauts that aren't capable of doing anything else or thinking about anything else, but when you take the possibility away it is amazing how it attacks your mind like an infectious disease. Hang in there though, the time will pass and you will be back into normal operations before too long. Well, an adjusted new normal operation. Did I mention it was 6 weeks? Just making sure. No really, six weeks. You actually have to watch a full calendar month roll off and some. To put that in perspective it would be like missing almost half a season of college football. A funny quote arrived through marriage and it goes like this; "it took marriage to ...." you fill in the blank.

Six weeks does funny things to the mind

Daniel- That's one view. Not all ladies lose their "interest" during their pregnancy. It'll just be a little different and more gentle. I was actually one of those guys that read the pregnancy books right alongside my wife. I was actually surprised to see the survey results that more often than not it's the guy that loses interest later in pregnancy and that many woman increase their interest. I had to chuckle when I read that one of the main fears of men is hurting the baby. Well, obviously there are limitations. And regardless of whether you believe in divine design or the Big Bang, at the very least, women have been having babies for at least 6 thousand years. Yeah, their bodies have figured out this whole pregnancy thing. But there is a truth to the 6 week after rule. And it can suck. But your lady needs to recover. So you find other avenues or routes to the end goal. Some women may have absolutely no interest in you other than to help out with the baby. Others may be a different story. So you work together to find ways "to be together" that doesn't violate the rules laid forth by the doctor.

To bring it all together, there is only one rule that is steadfast. It is the same rule that applies when dating or any other life situation. No means no and even maybe is sometimes no. Let your lady dictate when her body is ready to fight the horny toad.

TOPIC 11
I LUV POOP

It does not matter how private you used to be in your manners of going to the bathroom, having children changes everything. Did you like peeing alone? Well, if you're lucky enough to have a son you will get the opportunity to pee fight in the epic battle of toilet wars.

Skyler-I tried to avoid this but one day my son figured out that if he sat by me and watched to learn, once I started going he would pull down his pants and start going too. "Daddy, look we are sword fighting" hahaha. I said no, we are pee fighting, sword fighting is something we never do!

Daniel-Yeah, um I have girls. I've got nothing to say to that.

Skyler- My wife tried to get our boys to sit down and pee...enough said, I'd rather have the pee fighting and occasional mess to the side of the toilet. Ahem, the occasional time they actual aim and get in the toilet I should say. Unless of course it's summer then to boys the world is our toilet...even apparently our BBQ.

Anyway that is just peeing, it gets better if you are trying to go poop and they walk in and want to see it, analyze it and tell you what you did. Although you may get the feeling of being proud because yes, you made it, it is still crap you are discussing.

"Look, two poops that have horns. Like unicorns dad." You will be amazed at what they see in turd shape images. The fun doesn't end there because when they go poop they are even more fascinated. "Look Daddy, this one is stinky." Or "look I put my hand in my butt and it stinks." Um, yeah, you bet it does. Or immediately after they go to the bathroom wanting to pick it up to see what it feels like. In some cases, like this one, we're glad as an adult we lose part of that imaginative child brain. Don't worry if you walk in to see poop drawings, brown rimmed toilet seats, or just missed turds that somehow managed to make it to the floor only to be stepped in. This is all part of the process.

Potty training is something we'll go more into in a future book. But yes, it's rather different to not only be talking about poop, but to try to help them understand that the pressure they feel is not a turtle head poking out. You gotta run to the john and get that thing out. And if Daddy doesn't hear a plop then it didn't happen.

OK, that is the easy part of pooping and children, now let's take it back a few years and talk about baby crap. The evolution of poop is amazing in humans. Here is the timeline:

Newborn crap- black; Infant crap- yellow mustard; Toddler crap- brown and nasty;

And with hopeful Daddy expectations you hope to never have to the deal with any blood. You are going to think as a new dad that all your kid does is eat, sleep, and poop and you will be right. It is amazing how many poopy diapers you will change in the first month. Scratch that, the first day! And if your child is anything like ours, they will have an innate ability to manage to fill their britches with especially pungent dukes when it is your turn to change them. And that's not all! You will actually be encouraged (especially if your wife has read the pregnancy books) to track how many wet and crap diapers the little factory produces each day!

During the day you won't mind changing the diapers. It is at 2 and 4 in the morning when you can barely open your eyes and you know that they have shite themselves, but you debate whether to let it go one more time or until morning to change them. Although you inevitably end up changing them out of pure guilt knowing you would be letting them fester in their own crap, it doesn't mean it doesn't cross your mind, it is normal.

In comes Desitin. This champion of poop-be-gone is the key to stopping diaper rash before it ever starts. It is actual butt paste.

Skyler- Somehow I pretend every time I put this stuff on that I am dressing my child up for war, like Braveheart. My child is the William Wallace of turd fighting once he gets his makeup on. Like the movie, you aren't putting on the butt paste for nothing. It is war, and the shit might not hit the fan in your life, but it will definitely be just about everywhere else.

Have wipes everywhere and some hand sanitizer. Screw the germs, that is a secondary benefit, those products are good for just getting the unimaginable off of your hands, clothes and hair.

It always amazes us that even though they are properly equipped with a diaper their ability to poop down their legs or straight up their back leaving the diaper virtually poop free. Think about the physics in that. At what speed does that crap have to be propelled to ricocheted off the diaper and up their back? That is the beauty of opening up a diaper. Every single time you never know what you're going to get. Kind of like a box of chocolates. Got to love surprises.

When changing the diaper, place another diaper underneath the one being changed, this will help you avoid getting any blowouts or crap on the carpet, blanket, changing area etc. Always have all your items ready before starting the change.

Diaper Genie or any poop receptacle is at best temporary solutions. These things smell like crap and should be changed often regardless of where you dispose your diapers. You're probably better off not using one at all! Sure, it's a pain to have to walk outside to dispose of the vile excrement each and every time it happens. But, if you offer to do that, there's only one other person to finish up the job! Now don't think that this will deduct Dad points, because it won't. What mother wants to go outside, at night, in the cold, with a stinky diaper that's oozing at the edges? Not many. Especially in the dead of winter. So you get out of putting that kid back to bed, but hero points for braving the snow at night to get the smell out of the house.

Handling myths: Yes, babies can actually shoot crap right out of there little butts while you are changing them. The crap cannon IS real. Yes, if you have boys they can pee on you, however they are better at peeing all over themselves and their faces if you don't watch them. This makes you have to change their clothes, which means more laundry, which means more work, which means, well, just be prepared. Girls, on the other hand, have the ability to pee without you really noticing and getting everything beneath them wet and you won't notice until you pick them up and "AH &*^#@!" the whole process starts again.

From Dude to Dad

TOPIC 12
DOLLAR STORE PEE STICKS

There are many ways to find out whether you and your lady are pregnant.

  * The denial method, hmm, she must be gaining weight cause we are lazy and eat a ton of food while watching TV for hours a day (even though you are active).

  * The Stick of Destiny, aka, the pee stick. Yep, just how it sounds. Your lady takes a little stick and pees on it. Plus sign or double lines your screwed or happy, minus sign and your either back to the drawing board or in a celebratory mood.

  * There's always the go to the doctor method for confirmation whether you are in denial or disbelief. Nothing like seeing a person in a white coat break the news, the reality really hits.

Whatever your method of choice is, be in a good spot to accept the news.

Dudes, this is your chance to be cheap. Pee sticks are sold at the dollar store and are just as accurate as the ones at any other store. In fact, they might even work better cause they know that you're purchasing them there so they damn well better be accurate. Don't buy condoms there, totally different. And for those who have never bought condoms they don't come in 60 packs and plastic bags, those are balloons.

Let's just tell you Skyler's 2 experiences with this.

The first time we found out we were pregnant Katie was taking about 50 pee sticks just to really confirm the disbelief we were going through. We were freshly married, and when I mean freshly we could practically feel the ocean breeze of the cruise we had just disembarked and conceived. We were not trying by any means to have a child. The stick brought forth the news we expected but not ready for, we were pregnant. Many tears came after, and those were just mine. Actually I was pretty stoked, but my wife, I believe, specifically told me in her own words that I ruined her life. Can you see that doing these types of tests are probably best when there is some time alone or at least a good spot?

Fast forward 3 years. This time we are also using the pee sticks (dollar store of course) and we continue to get the negative sign. No, I didn't forget how we did it the first time. It was that this time we were trying to get pregnant. Time and time again we were disappointed to not be pregnant as we wanted our kids to be close together in age. Finally about 20 pee sticks in and over a year later we did it. The superhuman sperm had found the egg. Come to find out 2 made it and we had our twins. Imagine that surprise when you go to an ultrasound and the doctor comes in and says there is your boy, there is your other boy, and continues with let me see what the third is...or at least that is what I thought, I about passed out at that point or at very least needed a change of underwear. Thankfully, the twins are all we found giving us a total of 3 boys.

Daniel's experience:

Luckily, my wife and I didn't have any surprise pregnancies, yet. We were married for two years before we decided to have her get off birth control and start trying. A year later, nothing. And that can be really upsetting when you're finally ready for one. It can be especially disheartening for your lady when month after month there's nothing while others around you get pregnant quickly. Or worse, the countless stories on the local news of the impoverished children born to deadbeat parents. Be prepared for tears from both of you there. We got to the point where we were evaluating the cost of fertility clinics or an adoption. At the same time, we found out my wife had a condition that required medication and without treatment was preventing pregnancies. After a full month of being on the medication, we tracked her cycle one more time and bam! we're pregnant. The second time around, a few years later, was almost as hard. Yeah, we're one of those couples that has to track everything to get pregnant. Her temperature, cycle, moon sign, you name it. But once we found the pattern, the next month we were pregnant. So you never know how it'll happen. Just be prepared.

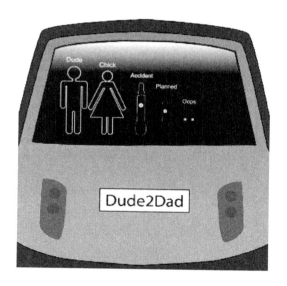

Dude's Notes: If you are expecting to have a child and it comes out positive this can be a great moment, celebrate. If you are trying to have a child and it comes out negative, plan an activity to take your mind off of it. If you don't want to have a child this can be a very tense moment. Analyze your situation and plan accordingly for the outcome. And by analyze, we mean you need to have a firm understanding of what your lady is really wanting.

TOPIC 13
WHAT'S YOUR LADY LIKE IN BED?

Bed check, how big is your bed? If you are use to a full, get a queen. If you are used to a queen, get a king. If you are used to a king, we hope you have a nice couch. It's not so much that the lady's belly gets so big you can't fit, it's all the other intangibles, or in this case very tangibles.

Covers Magician: This is the pregnant lady that makes the covers disappear. You can wake up 4 times at night and still not have covers. Tuck them in, nail them down, press your leg on it, it doesn't matter. Pregnant women can have you coverless in the blink of an eye.

The Rolley Poley: This is the lady that slowly rotates back and forth all night long rolling back and forth.

Ninja Chop: Like all good ninjas you never see these strikes of fury coming. Some people do this without being pregnant.

Just hope you get chopped somewhere where you can get back to sleep and not be in too much pain.

Pee Burglar: This is the lady that needs to get up and pee every other half hour and wakes you up because you think someone is coming into your room. This one also makes you have to pee way more often as you are up and hear the sound.

Leg Wrestler: This one doesn't come as furious as the Ninja Chop, but can be still an unwanted challenge at night. This is the lady that can't hold her legs still and wants to constantly leg wrestle you as if her legs will magically rub against you and your magical leg hairs will somehow settle hers down.

The Furnace: This is opposite to the Covers Magician. Daniel's wife is almost always cold so she always wants to snuggle. Until she's in the later months of pregnancy. Recall the adage, "she's got a bun in the oven." Boy, does she ever. Not to be insulting on size, but it's like a potbellied stove. It can heat and heat and heat and you get it, heat. And covers trap that in. So that made Daniel's wife happy. But he's a hot sleeper and was very uncomfortable during those months. Luckily, his two children were born in the late summer so his wife actually got to the point of wanting the AC cranked way up.

Moral of the section, say goodbye to decent sleep now. It's preparation for what's to come.

TOPIC 14
THE THREE LEGGED GIRL

An ultrasound is one of the coolest times of transition from Dude to Dad. Let us start by saying, DO NOT MISS this opportunity to see and hear for the first time your newborn.

Skyler's experience with ultrasounds:

1st ultrasound, it's a girl.

2nd ultrasound, it's a boy.

Daniel's:

1st -girl, very obviously a girl.

There's no going back once you've been claimed a boy...unless you're a girl with three legs or eleven fingers.

100 percent do not miss your chance to experience this amazing feeling. Take work off, take life off, make it to this appointment if you can only make it to one. Not another

thing will measure up to that very moment they bring your child up on the screen for you to view. Also it will be a moment that you and your lady can share forever. This moment is the stuff life is made of, or at least the stuff that means something. I guarantee you can be a hard-core son of bitch with as many tattoos as you want and when you see a little foot, a little hand, or the heart beating you will become as gooey as the Pillsbury Dough Boy. Don't worry we won't tell, in fact we encourage it. We don't have to be bad ass all the time and I know that this will punch you harder in the heart strings than any person has punched you in a fight.

This is your only warning. There is nothing in this life or the next that can make up for missing the ultrasound.

TOPIC 15
SPORTS CARS AND STATION WAGONS

This is a tense moment.

Skyler- My driving up until having a baby was more like a NASCAR driver looking for the checkered flag. It is a total 180 within 48 hours. Why a 180? When your lady goes in labor you think you are a champion because your NASCAR driving pays off when having to rush to the hospital. For me her contractions were happening every 7 minutes. I quickly did the math and realized if I didn't fly through the streets and arrive at the hospital precisely in 18 minutes I was going to have to endure an extra contraction. Which I know my pain was nothing like hers, but it was like talons of a hawk grabbed my hand and gave a death squeeze. Add this to trying to drive and it was not a fun situation. So, the race began. We did arrive before a 3rd contraction happened and my nail-dug arm was grateful. That was going to the hospital. Fast forward to after baby delivery and heading home. It was as if someone replaced my race car with a station wagon and you could barely see my knuckles over the steering wheel. I suddenly became an old man driving like my car had a walking stick. 15 miles an hour on a 40 mile an hour street is more dangerous but for some reason I thought if I drove fast my child would magically launch through the windshield in a torpedo fashion with his car seat. Don't ask me, but that first drive home, expect a total change in your typical driving habits. It feels a lot like every other car is out to get you. Kind of like Pac-man. You're trying to clear a board or get home and every other car is like the ghosts trying to make you crash and have game over.

Daniel- The first time around, my wife woke us at 3 something in the morning because her water broke. The hospital was only a half mile away so I didn't have to rush. The second time, we waited a little too long. I almost couldn't even get her to the hospital. I think I drove fairly quickly. But my wife was mad I wasn't driving in the oncoming side of the road just to pass people. We got to the hospital and literally two minutes later had our second child.

From Dude to Dad

TOPIC 16
IT'S ALL ABOUT THE MONEY

Dear new parent,

You will be billed a bill, but not the first three
The real bill will be the bill that Doctor Bill charges,
We will tell you what we will bill, then bill the <u>billers</u> to bill
you,
Everyone will get their shot at writing a different bill to
confuse the hell out of you.
Don't worry this is all part of the process and we assure you
that We, your insurance company will get our money.

From, Your insurance.

Here's the deal. The idea of insurance is great but they have
gone so far off the deep end of what it was originally created
for it can make you sick, to be fair it's not just them, it is how

doctors bill, pharmaceuticals, and the list goes on and on. The important thing to know is it is a business and to be wise about your purchase there are precautions you can take like making sure you check all your statements when the onslaught of bill descriptions and actual bills start coming in the mail. They will take a while to come, but once they start they'll never stop. Make sure you are not overpaying either, many bills might be delayed and it is easy to end up paying one and then having to try to get reimbursed which is about as fun as getting a tooth extracted (which will be another insurance bill for dental, equally as painful). The other tip when it comes to getting your bills reduced is to set up payment plans. This will show your willingness to pay off the bill. After making one payment, call in and see if you can get a discount if you pay the bill off in full that day. You can often get 20 to 30 percent off the price especially in hospitals because they get stiffed so often they would rather have that cash in hand. That is big bucks if you have the ability to pay it off in full.

Doctors are awesome, people running hospitals, clinics and insurance companies also have great intentions, but there is a reason it is a trillion dollar industry.

From Dude to Dad

TOPIC 17
PUSSIES AND DOGGY STYLE

Do you already have animals together? Have you thought about animals together? Have you never even spoken a word in your life about animals together? This sounds like it is going to be some big explanation starting with so many questions, but really it is simple. Decide right now, before or after you have already had your child on how many animals you would like in your household. Skyler thought of himself typically as a one animal type person, so he and his wife adopted a cat. Great cat, wouldn't trade her for the world. Note to Dudes, pregnant women cannot empty cat litter, kind of like single dudes can't do laundry. Sure they can, it's just not safe. Anyway, back to the point. Skyler is now outnumbered by his kids and wife and feels his house is slowly turning into a zoo. They have a cat and 3 fish tanks and the newest beast of the household is a golden retriever.

Skyler- I like animals, I just wish they weren't purchased on whims of hormones, children, or any other less stable ways of making long term commitments. Plus I am not Beastmaster (If you don't know what Beastmaster is now is good time to watch this classic).

So talk about your animal situation early and often so that you end up having animals to take care of not having animals you are stuck with. Make sure you have family commitments to taking care of these life forms that depend on you for survival. Sure man's best friend, but man doesn't necessarily want 5 best friends.

From Dude to Dad

TOPIC 18
SHAPE SHIFTER

Here's the deal. Her body is going to go through some extreme changes. Much like an X-Men character that has the ability to shape shift. It doesn't matter if she looks like she grew a mustache and her legs look like she is an Amazon woman, she has your child and chances are the baby is going to come out looking just like her body changes.

Skyler- My wife grew tuffs of red hair that looked like little horns. I thought I was either having the spawn of Satan or my son would be red-headed. Sure enough the first thing to come out the day of delivery was this full head of red-hair.

Of course there is the normal stretch of the belly and largeness, but there are so many other things that can and do happen. Have you ever read one of those books that you can match the different sections of bodies? The head, torso, and legs are all different so you can mix and match or find the complete set. Just pretend this is one of those opportunities. Even better take pictures of your lady and create your own book to mix and match and then just plan on sleeping on the couch that night cause that is where you will be headed, but hey, if she is at the end stages of pregnancy it might just be a better place to get sleep, plus you'll have a sweet book.

TOPIC 19
IT'S ALIIIIIVE!

There is definitely a difference here between when the Dad sees the first movements and the mom. The mom feels movement from the baby a bit earlier and the sensation is different.

Example:

The mother: A small gaseous feeling occurs. The sensation is different than normal gas though and the soon to be mom instinctively knows this is her baby. Awwweeee, I can feel the baby move.

The first time us Dudes recognize we have a baby:
It's aaaaaliiiiiive.

It really does look like some random claw trying to crawl out of your beautiful lady's belly. She has been taken over, it's official, she will never be just yours anymore. It's almost like a wave good-bye to what used to be. It also might be the baby's way of creeping you out just for fun. If you have a camera, which in today's day and age you probably do, take the time to get this on camera. It really is pretty trippy and you will want to watch it over and over again just because it is unbelievable. Whether you see it as your first alien encounter or nice moment, sit back and enjoy, being a dad is cool.

Skyler- I am pretty sure when we were having our twin boys they were destined to be synchronized swimmers, then I just realized they were already fighting in the womb as they love to do now. Imagine that cage fight, there is no escape.

TOPIC 20
THE PINK BARF ROBE

Skyler- I wake up to the sound of throw up,

Almost like an alarm clock every morning.

Tired in my state of being I ask my wife.

"Would you like some cheerios?"

She looked at me like I was more disgusting then the vomit that just exited her mouth.

"NO."

Morning sickness is like the equivalent of having a constantly sick person in the house without the ailment of being sick.

I have never been puking and then right after ask for a roast beef sandwich with pickles.

There is only one cure for morning sickness and that is TIME. Try to do your best to support her any way you can. Get brave enough to hold your wife's hair back as she throws up, how is that for love. (Dad points +1000)

Though it is called morning sickness the label doesn't really stay true to all women. They might get sick in the evening and the sickness also varies. It could be they just get really tired. Dudes know that you may get tired taking a dump, but to need to nap immediately after seems a bit extreme. With any luck your lady won't get sick, although some women claim in some ways it has benefit because she didn't balloon up in weight as the cravings kicked in.

Our advice is to have some sort of soda like Sprite or Ginger Ale on hand and a few types of crackers like Saltines just in case. The key here is that they always need to have something in their stomach. Keep a stash of food in every room of the house if you have to and at the bare minimum by her side of the bed. During this time it is perfect to implement the flower plan and write a simple note letting her know you appreciate the sacrifices she is making and what she is going through. Or go with the lighter side and just say "I am glad you are my BFF (Barf Friend Forever). See how this will score a million more points than on a holiday. That is called chalking one down in a woman's memory bank.

Instead of flowers Skyler chose to make up for his offering of Cheerios in the worst time by getting her a nice soft pink barfing robe, every girl needs one. Well, it's a normal soft pink robe that she could stay warm in while she barfs.

From Dude to Dad

TOPIC 21
ETCH A SKETCH BODY

When Dudes think of our bodies we think of the subtle and not so subtle changes that occur in ourselves. For most of us we are much like an Etch a Sketch, shake us up out of our routine and it is easy to see all our lines or muscle definition fade quickly.

Skyler- When my wife got pregnant with our first child and then about a ½ a year after delivery I gained about 25 pounds. Granted going into the pregnancy I was in very good shape. It is easy to want to give up and eat your way through a pregnancy, especially because your lady will be eating like every minute is more like a buffet snack line. This is not a diet book and I am not a dietician. You want to be a fat ass dad or just a little chubbier then usual than have at it. This is more of a coffee wake up call to let you know it's not always a choice and it can just sneak up on you. I know 25 pounds is more of a blob than something than sneaks up on you, but it does. Because you are looking at yourself all the time and are constantly busy with your new freaked out emotions of becoming a dad, reality as it used to be gets sort of side-lined. So this is your moment to make an effort to stay in shape through thick and thin sort to speak. Because your lady is going to get thick, it's your choice whether you stay thin (not supermodel throw up thin, in shape, or if you are still wanting to maintain your muscles that landed you that girl, those too)

Daniel- Of course, you can call it sympathy weight. "Look hun, I was X lbs heavier than you before. I'm just keeping that up."

Skyler- Now fast forward three and half years and my wife is pregnant with twins. Yes twins. That is a whole different book I will write later called "How to sacrifice all sleep and time and still be living". I approached the second pregnancy with a different mindset that I was going to stay in shape as I was older and my metabolism has definitely shifted against me. I can't just do a few push up and sit ups and watch the six-pack reappear. Here is my strategy. It is simple, cut out all the steak and potatoes you are eating, drop the beer and soda, and focus on fresh veggies and drinking lemon water. Buy a thighmaster, ab cruncher and don't forget the space saving treadmill and work out just 6 days a week for 2 hours a day and send me 80 dollars a week for the program. You will be in fantastic shape guaranteed! My real strategy is called opportunistic eating and exercise. I don't like veggies myself so I found some great ways to fake my body into thinking I was eating them. Get ready for it, I drink every day some Amazing Grass Outrageous Chocolate drink. They load it with organic fruits and veggies and it tastes like drinking chocolate milk. I then upped my manly levels by getting Animal Parade Kid Greenz chewables. I eat one of those every morning and I drink the chocolate milk later in the day. That is the only diet changes I made. The only other thing I can recommend because I have such a bad habit of it is if you are going to eat ice cream or shakes, eat them earlier in the day. I love drinking them at night before bedtime. So there is the diet, one veggie chewable and one veggie/fruit drink.

The opportunistic portion of eating comes in like this, if you aren't craving it and can resist at any time of the day do. Yep, if you crave it and can't withstand, eat it, if you can, don't.

Exercise. Remember this book is about Daddyhood, not a solve all fitness program. I am letting you know what I did in hopes it will help you too. If you are in the gym all the time or any type of hard core athlete you will need to research another way. But for the average dude, this is good stuff. Opportunistic exercise. Buy a pull up bar. That is the one piece I will say is a must buy. Put it in one of your doorways of your house. Every time you go through that door do two pull ups. With every pull up do a leg lift with it. If you can't do any, hang on the bar, if you can do more, great. The key is every time you go through that door you must do at least two or your best effort. You will be amazed how much strength is accumulated through just that alone. Do you have stairs in your house? Your work? Always take stairs and every stair you step on extend your calf muscle up, if there is only one or two stairs, maybe do a few calf raises each time you pass the stairs. When I brush my teeth, the whole time I am brushing my teeth a do knee raises to work my abs. Sometimes to the side, other times straight up to my stomach. If I am ever laying down, I do two push-ups to get up instead of just standing up. It's all about getting your mind to take advantage of using energy where you can. That is why it isn't a fitness program, it is an opportunistic program that maximizes your normal routine. Once your child is born, start incorporating them into your exercises. Lift them up and down as you hold them, to the side. They like the swinging motion, you get the benefits. As they grow older I have my son lay on my back while we watch cartoons and I do a few push-ups. Then have him sit on my legs and I lift him working my abs and my legs. He loves this and we bond, I benefit too. As you start to incorporate some of these ideas you will see that you look for more ways to add to your movement and increase the amount of exercise you are getting naturally.

TOPIC 22
MIND GAMES

Most of the time you see the word "game" and you think, sounds fun. And then you put the word "mind" in front of it and it changes the feeling completely. Now you think, controlling, or perhaps uncontrolled. You may think you are totally sound in your mind right now, but we have seen the process of pregnancy and Daddyhood tear down even the strongest of minds. There is something that clicks that is sometimes scary, sometimes just to foreign that overwhelms the body causing a breaking point. Having this book is a great resource to help aid through any tough times.

Skyler- I had never felt anxiety before. In fact, I knew it was a term but thought people were just over reacting to situations. I remember clearly one night as we were nearing the end of my wife's pregnancy with our first child having a near out of body experience that later I found out was anxiety. My mind went so far ahead into the future that I was 60 had my kids grown up and was a grandpa and my life was over and it happened within a second. I never had felt that way before, something just clicked and I was out of it. I researched much about what had happened, much to the inspiration of why I am writing this book, to help us dudes out in realizing much of what happens to us and what we can do as we enter Daddyhood.

Daniel- I actually have anxiety quite often. When my second child was born, it happened so quickly that I didn't have time to be freaked out on the drive to the hospital. In fact, when I had to run home after the delivery to get the rest of what my wife needed to feel comfortable, I was experiencing the panic of not making it to the hospital in time and had to remind myself that the baby was already here safe and sound.

Obviously there is a wealth of knowledge out on the web, but we can narrow what gave Skyler peace of mind down to one book. Eckartt Tolle's A New Earth. (For Daniel it was his Dad reminding him that mankind has been doing this for so long it's the oldest and most known branch of medicine so chill out.)

Skyler- It smacked me back into the moment and helped me stay there to focus on the life I needed to be living instead of what could happen in the future or what did happen in the past.

Don't worry about what your parents did or didn't do, what mistakes you made in your past or will make in your future, live the right now and start and end right there. Maybe it will be this book that allows you a more fit mind. But realize your mindset will change, there will be challenges and you will be fine. Especially if you were a hellion as a child and were wondering if your child would be back to torture you as you did your parents.

Keep this book around as a quick guide to ease and strengthen your mind that you are one of the many Dudes going through the same thing and are not alone.

From Dude to Dad

TOPIC 23
RANSACKING OPPORTUNIST

Our grandparents are great at illustrating what to do as you leave the hospital. Because they grew up in the great depression they are excellent savers and don't like to waste anything. They are also keen on being opportunists when it comes to free stuff.

Skyler- I have a great image of my Nana and the family going to a buffet. We were all stuffed and getting ready to leave when I watched her go to the dessert bar and snag several donuts, put them in napkins and placed them in her purse. It always made me smile cause she wanted the most for her money, and had an insatiable sweet tooth.

The hospital is the same way. You are checked in there and have already made a commitment to having to pay for your stay, so you might as well get what you can to help you. With Skyler's first son he didn't leave with a single thing from their stay, just kind of happy to leave the hospital in general and more concerned with getting home safely. With his twins they had great nurses that told us to load up on all the things we could because you would have to buy enough stuff anyway so you might as well get a good start. Excellent idea. With Daniel's first, the nurse opened their bag and stuffed more stuff into it.

Of course these items aren't going to save the family farm so to speak in finances, but every bit helps. Take home several packages of diapers, wipes, loads of butt paste, saline and a bulb syringe for sucking boogers out, some nice little wash cloths, loads of sponges for baths, mini bottles, water cups to heat the bottles in, and much more. Look around you in your room and see what is available. Ask a nurse what they can send you home with. Each child will be different as you stay at the hospital will vary depending if you have a child born early, on time, with complications or not. But one thing is for sure, there are things available, especially when you ask. If one nurse says there isn't, ask another, it is amazing what the right nurse can do.

TOPIC 24
TAKE-OUT OR DELIVERY

Not to be confused with a pizza delivery or Chinese takeout, unless of course your doctor is from China and he is about to take something out. Brace yourself for this day fellow dudes. There are several different options we will take you through during this phase of Daddyhood. Now keep in mind there are others such as home delivery (for those brave souls who enjoy not having modern medicine at their side), and the unexpected delivery in a car, plane or some other God forbidden place. Our focus is the hospital delivery, as this is where most babies are born. First of all, congratulations if you are in the hospital with your wife and you in one piece, that journey is one hell of a car ride. Your wife can have a C-section or Vaginal delivery. Let's talk about both to have you better prepared for whatever your eyes are about to see.

Vaginal Delivery- normally when you put the word vagina in a sentence as a man your ears are a little more attentive. And also normally when the word vagina is in a sentence it can be associated with something good (unless you are a gynecologist). Mark my words, vaginal delivery is the closest thing you will see to watching a bloody horror show about an alien being taken out of its host's body. Don't worry it isn't the best for them either, it's not every day you get about 2 different people every hour coming in and prodding you with fingers to see if/how far they have effaced. Not to mention the Batman like spot light that lights up your lady's nether region like never before. We know, we hate to ruin the awe inspiring beautiful factors of life being born. But really, it is a bloody mess and it starts with the vagina expanding to watch a head of hair (or bald) crown.

Skyler -As my wife dilated I could actually feel my own anus puckering in pain due to the massive stretching taking place.

Don't worry because having a child is an active process. The nurses will get you in on the action like your lining up on defense to sack the quarterback. You will have your lady's leg bent out, up, touching the back of her head, whatever, and once in position it's like holding down the Kracken's tentacles if they don't have an epidural. In your mind you are thinking, I should have taken a birthing class and I am going to tell you they don't teach the shit that happens in the delivery room anyway. Oh, epidural, before we forget, is a drug they give your lady so that you can relax and not have any extremities ripped off. It's also a great drug for the lady too. Are we over reacting, yeah, maybe. But we can only go off our experiences and the crowning is just the start to what takes place next. You will see your little miracle child continue to sneak his way into the world like spelunking his way out of a dark cavern until his shoulders are through and this is precisely when the rest of their body pops out with the rest of whatever is left inside. What might you see in this process? Good question. Of course blood, but you will also see a ton of other fluid along with the placenta. (Total side topic and kind of sick, remember this image, it will come in handy when you have your 6 week drought after delivery)

Skyler- In my case I was treated to what I would consider a Yellowstone type geyser of blood that literally spurted out. Not saying it will happen, but it can.

Alright baby is out, lady is exhausted, now what? Nobody told Skyler that a baby doesn't necessarily breathe within the first 20 seconds after being pushed through the canal. Do not freak out if you have a baby and the doctor is counting into and past the minute mark or even two.

Skyler- I was told after I was almost passed out, weak kneed and trembling in tears that up to about 4 to 5 minutes everything is usually just fine and no damage occurs. Everything, I mean everything at the very moment your child makes their first little cry into the world disappears and a magical euphoria comes over you staring at a child you have never met. It is amazing that a connection can be made without ever seeing, touching, or interacting with your child. Take in the moment, cause it's not like your drunken one night stand where you told the girl you had never met there was an amazing connection with her just to get some action, but the feeling remains the same and is hard to remember once it is gone.

And dudes, that is a vaginal delivery. Side notes: bring food and drinks for yourself. Delivery times vary but you don't want to die of hunger while supporting your lady. Make sure you hide it though, cause they aren't allowed to eat. So avoid food that is really fragrant. Unless of course it is the playoffs, bring in the BBQ turn on the free cable in the hospital and enjoy the game! Quiz for you. If you knew you were going to be kicked in the nuts would you take something that would make you completely numb so you couldn't feel it? Epidural, it will make your whole experience much easier on you and your lady.

C-Section- this type of delivery is completely different and can happen for many reasons. Sometimes they are scheduled, sometimes they are emergencies.

Skyler- I don't know if you have ever seen a surgery take place but for some reason in my mind I thought of how fragile they must be with every little incision and cut they do to our delicate bodies. Hmmm. I was wrong. It was like watching a strong man competition with two heavy weight champions pulling my wife's mid-section in opposite directions. First the gentle incision, more like a steak knife carving out a piece of rough beef.

A C-section is your only chance to actually get to see if your lady is as beautiful on the inside as she is on the outside. As they cut into each layer till getting to the guts it is an interesting eyeful to watch them actually place her innards onto her outtards. Not to use the tentacle analogy again, but they grabbed a foot and it was very much octopus like. That was, of course, until they pulled the rest of the baby out.

Skyler-They yanked 'em out, grabbed his waist and neck and showed the bloody little guy to my wife and I as if to say, "look what I did" then swiftly took him away for cleaning and vitals. For us the C-section was far more relaxed than the water breaking unexpectedly then rushing to the hospital. We checked into the hospital, went over the procedure and side effects then calmly went back to the operating room. We were even able to get a few requests in for my wife to make it more enjoyable for her. Once the baby is pulled out, they dump a ton of saline down into your lady, much like flushing out a system to give a nice little wash before playing an operation like game and putting all the pieces back. I got the privilege of having my doctor compliment and show me my wife's ovaries that were still on her stomach region. Jot that one down as good to know.

The C-section will take longer to heal from so be extra sensitive to your lady's needs as she will need it. Whatever you do, don't ask your doctor to write your initials as she is sewing her back up, it just isn't right. And no, Skyler didn't think about it, he heard about someone trying to do this and even worse a doctor who put his own initials.

Daniel- I've mentioned some of our experiences briefly in previous sections. My wife delivered vaginally both times. And both times it looked extremely painful with lots of blood. I'm still amazed how often a birth happens and how rare it really is to have loss of life in the whole process. The first time was very slow. Her water broke at 3 something in the morning and we went to the hospital and waited and waited until our daughter finally decided to come out at 1 in the afternoon.

Our second was quite quick. We got to the hospital and I ran in for a wheel chair. They looked for an orderly to do it and I said, pointing to an empty chair behind their desk, "I'm fully capable of pushing a wheel chair. Just give me that one." So they did and I ran it out to the car where my wife was screaming that her water just broke. I tried to cheer her up by saying that now the hospital won't send us home (they already had a few times). I had to literally lift her out of the car and into the wheel chair. The baby was crowning by this point. Sounds exactly as it is. Their head is poking out. So my wife was holding herself up on the arm rests. We get up to the maternity wing, scream our way into a room, and in two minutes, I've hoisted her onto the bed and baby is out and cord is cut. I'm not kidding either. Literally two minutes from the entrance to the hospital to baby. Yep. Talk about adrenaline.

Delivery is like the Russian Roulette of Daddyhood, you just never know what to expect as anything can happen. Always focus on the best positive outcome no matter what you have heard or are hearing. Doctors and Nurses often tell you every possibility, as it is their job, but sometimes you just don't want to hear about all the negative things that can happen. If it happens, deal with it then. Life is good, being there for your lady during this amazing time is essential, don't miss out on this opportunity to welcome your little one to this world and support your lady.

From Dude to Dad

TOPIC 25
THE LONE RANGER

It is amazing, up until this very moment in life you have never wanted the in-laws, normal family or friends around for extended stays at your house as it invaded your alone time and your sexy time. But now, now is different. Like the Lone Ranger you will enter a night alone eventually without the securities of others, some quicker than others. If you have a network of family or friends you will get to this first night completely alone probably later in the first or second week of your child's life rather than immediately leaving the hospital. Whenever this day comes, transformation occurs.

Skyler- I would like to think I am a solid capable dude, but my mind wasn't prepared correctly for sleepless walking zombie diaper changing throwing up on Dad the first night alone. Up until then there was someone to ask or help do the baby things that baby things need to be done. But this night is different, a crying baby that will not stop has got to be the most gut wrenching helpless feeling one can feel.

Be prepared for this day. It's like watching your favorite sports team all season long deep into the playoffs only to have them win it all or lose either way it is all over that next night. Something is missing and you can feel it. What is being prepared? If your baby is bottle fed, have that ready. If you have work in the morning, go to sleep extra early to compensate for the time you will be up all night. Get a good light that isn't too bright, but bright enough to allow you to comfortably change a diaper without sticking your hand in crap. Get a little radio to plays some soft songs or lullaby's for your child while you rock them. Have as many things readily available as you can while your brain is functioning cause at 2, 4, and 5 in the morning it is much more difficult. By being there for that night means you are a good dad.

Daniel- It is also entirely normal to be completely freaked out about the whole concept and be afraid to even breathe for fear you'll wake mother and baby and then they're both screaming at you. It's also normal that you want to check on the baby every few seconds to make sure they haven't stopped breathing on your watch. Again, totally normal and quite endearing to your wife when she's awake enough to think it's cute.

TOPIC 26
HUNGRY, LIKE THE WOLF

If you are from the 80's 90's or just love a great classic song you know what it's like to be hungry like a wolf. But what you may not know is what it is like to be hungry like a pregnant lady. You crave whatever crazy concoction you want, but please stop craving food from fast food places that are closed. We're okay with the crazy cravings and bizarre eating habits of pregnant women. It is actually a chance to broaden your food horizons. Have you ever even considered putting detergent on a sandwich? We wouldn't go that far, however, many pregnant ladies actually would do this if it wouldn't kill them as they do crave things of that nature. But eating a pickle split, you betcha, substitute a banana with a pickle and enjoy that concoction. Like we said, the part that killed us the most is when they would crave an Arby's roast beef sandwich approximately 5 minutes before they would close giving us no chance in hell to get there in time to cure the craving. And because we didn't possess these magical powers to behold an Arby's sandwich we were some kind of failure to society for at least that moment and mood. Luckily for us, in that instance, mood swings do occur as she was like a dog distracted by a squirrel when the TV came on with some cute baby items. And they say the T.V. takes away from family time.

Skyler- This inconvenient craving for an Arby's sandwich happened 2 more times before I took action. I went there and bought 5 sandwiches to have in the fridge ready for the occasion. Like a little kid just waiting to surprise her when she got that craving again, I just waited... and waited... and waited. Guess how many times she craved Arby's after I bought the sandwiches and hid them in the fridge? Yep, Zero. The sandwiches went bad.

Cravings are pretty much a non-winning situation as they are just that, spontaneous cravings. You can try to anticipate the next choice of randomness, however, my recommendation is to just sit tight, take the order when it comes in and do what you can to fulfill it. Satisfied cravings can equal freedom to watch your game uninterrupted, and just maybe if you bring it home with a nice card with something humorous or kind about the craving(remember, utilize their sensitive emotion to your favor) some loving. Feel free to try some of the cravings or make light of it by having some cravings of your own. You want to do something special for your lady and score the mega points here's what to do. Before any crazy cravings even set in, set up a living room picnic (blanket on your living room floor). Make a centerpiece (something you place in the middle of the blanket) with the most random thing you can find in your house. Then make a crazy lunch to eat. This will set the right tone to letting her know you understand what is about to come and that you are here to do your best. Besides you will have fun creating the menu items to eat that day. Example menu items can be taken from the below Menu for Pregnant Ladies.

From Dude to
Dad

Menu for pregnant chicks

Appetizer -

- Carrots dipped in caramel
- Small bowl of Lucky Charms
- Apple slices with honey
- Shredded cheese

Main Course -

- Macaroni and Cheese
- Ramen Noodles mixed with whatever you want
- Tuna fish gravy and toast
- Nachos (again put random toppings on with some normal and some abnormal)
- Buy one item from lots of different fast food places and have them in the different bags (a burrito from Taco Bell, a Snack Wrap from KFC, a McDonalds burger and some Panda Orange Chicken)

Dessert -

- Pickle split (ice cream and pickles) not for the faint at heart
- Sprinkles and whip cream on a bagel
- A chocolate chip pancake
- Honey butter and crackers

TOPIC 27
THE DUNK TANK

Have you ever seen those tanks full of water where people will sit on a plank and let people throw balls at a target that when hit will drop the plank and dunk you. Yeah, a dunking tank. The water breaking is like the reverse process of this. All these fluids are surrounding your baby and in your lady. Unfortunately there is no real target except for the due date as to when this process will occur. But when it does, it happens fast and unexpected and yes it is like a plank just got released and instead of your lady falling into the water, all the water falls out.

Skyler- We made the mistake of thinking my wife's water broke with our first child so we went into the hospital to get it checked out. Not a mistake we will make again. Aside from the nice cost associated with going in my wife had to endure a dry run. A dry run is getting checked with no lube to find out what is going on up there. Now, I was not the one getting checked, and I am not a pain management doctor but I was fairly certain by my wife's contorted face in pain that it was not a pleasantry that we would be repeating any time soon. The scream probably gave it away that it hurt too. But this section isn't about the dry run, it is about the water breaking.

Fast forwarding several weeks. My wife is having contractions, it is 3 in the morning. (Of course it isn't right after my cup of coffee and newspaper reading, no I am dreaming soundly.) We get up and cruise to the hospital. Without many details we get to the hospital and she is on the table and her water breaks. Like the ocean had just channeled a tsunami rogue wave water gushed out on to the table on to the floor. What the hell was that? I asked. Her water broke.

Rewind back to the weeks earlier, hahaha, laughing at ourselves for confusing a few drops of water for this gigantic wave of water.

Now we know this experience can vary from person to person, but we would bet that more often than not you will know for certain when the water breaks. Avoid the costly and painful in many ways dry run.

Daniel: The comforting thing about the water breaking is that the hospital will not send you away if it has legitimately broken. What do I mean by that? Yeah, they'll swab your lady's bits to test if the fluid really was amniotic fluid and not, I don't know, pee? Apparently they have to check that the sac actually broke instead of just leaked a little. Both labors I was like "Um, take a bottle of water and dump it out. That's what it was like." I guess the nurses just expect us dudes to exaggerate.

TOPIC 28
THE BRIEF CASE TRANSACTION

Remember when fanny packs were cool? Wrong, they never were. Hip packs, maybe, but fanny packs never. This is the same strategy with carrying around a diaper bag. Now you can just not carry one around, but this gets to be a pain in the butt trying to find all the things you need every time you leave the house or your car. Do I really care how cool I am? Not really. I think more for me it is just trying to not attract attention to myself like the dude in black socks, short shorts, and a muscle T at the gym working out. That same dude is probably the one that busts out on his way out of the gym a double zipping fanny pack that stores protein bars. Anyway, there is a lot of crap to hall around after having a baby if you don't want to be inconvenienced.

Skyler- My choice was finding a nice laptop case and organizing it like it was my business bag. Then when I had to change a poopy (yes I just said poopy I am a Dad, I can say that word) diaper I do it like a professional transaction. This diaper feels heavy and slightly smells. I estimate that will need 2 wipes, a fresh diaper, and because it is the fourth diaper in I swear what seems like diarrhea fairy land, I will need one squirt of angelic white Butt Paste. Check off the items as I pull them out in order to replace such items later at home. Finish the change, wrap up the old diaper, toss it in a trash and close the transaction. Baby is smiling, customer is happy, strap back down my bag and bam, I just helped fill the landfill with more literal shit. I'm not really proud of that, but cloth diaper alternatives, no thanks. I have invented several different products that help eliminate the diaper receptacles. As far as saving the Earth, I do what I can to recycle, but until there is an option better than scraping the turd off a cloth several times a day, sorry.

Look around your house for some of your old bags that can be your diaper bag. We guarantee you that you won't even care if you end up taking your lady's purse as long as you are living by the boy scout motto "be prepared."

TOPIC 29
EDU-FREAK-ATION

Tell us if this would help you out. You are learning to drive a car. You take 6 weeks of classes each week to learn all about these sweet sports cars with all the nice features. You even practice out in a safe parking lot the perfect gear shifts so you can easily get the car to perform at its highest level without ruining it. You baby the car to make it look perfect for that first ride. After 6 weeks your expectations are high, you're nervous because you don't want to stall the car or wreck it so you start going over each step in your mind on how to shift, how to start it up and turn it off. The day arrives, you get to the garage where this beautiful ride has been kept and...and an automatic station wagon with wood siding is there. You're already running late, your date is waiting. You throw it in gear and off you go.

Long story, short translation. The baby classes tell you all these ways a birth can happen from perfect natural delivery, to breathing, to blah blah blah. The only thing the classes did was scared the hell out of Skyler because it made him realize just how little he knew about all the things that take place and can go wrong or need to happen.

Skyler- With my first son, we showed up at an ungodly hour in the morning after not sleeping, they threw us in a room and before I could recover my arm from my wife ripping it off they had an epidural in her. Six hours later, all my preparation and mind work of what I needed to do was thrown out the door and my proverbial station wagon arrived. The nurse told me to essentially grab her leg like a football, push her knee into her skull and don't let go.

Sure the classes teach you great techniques and other great skills, but the reality is it freaks your mind out so bad that the messages are really that clear and rarely do the actions from the class get translated to the delivery. The exception to this is if you are crazy and your lady wants to give birth at home with a midwife. Not that it is a bad idea, it's just like throwing out your cell phone and computer and telling me you would prefer to type your message and send it in the mail. Sure it works and it is probably more personal, but again personally it would have been the difference between our wife's and child's life.

Daniel- Of course you can skip the classes all together. Well, not you alone. My wife and I didn't take them. We talked to her doctor about what to expect, read the book, and talked to siblings who already had kids. And now you can read our book as well.

TOPIC 30
I THINK WE SHOULD JUST BE FRIENDS

This phenomenon is like the same one that takes place when your parents tell you that you will understand when you have your own kids. It sounds stupid, until the change takes place. Here is my best interpretation of what happens in the cycle of friends. When you are single, you hang out with other single people. Then, some of your friends start to get married. You hang out with them for a little while, but much less often as you see them start to hang out with their other married friends. They start to collect other married friends and now you are the fifth wheel to what seems like all couples yet you are still friends so you make the time. Next, you have a child. All of a sudden you have two levels of separation with single people. Like the dinosaurs they have entered their own ice age and though you know they exist the sightings are a rarity. Making things more difficult you now face the fading married couples who have no kids because you have now become a little more like a chore to hang out with then the honeymooners free flow. Going out to eat you draw attention, need special accommodations, etc. making you a little less appealing to married couples and extremely less appealing to singles. You now focus your energy on finding other people with kids. This is a problem as it is hard to find couples with only one kid. You are now behind because the ones with multiple kids will always tell you how easy it is for you and it was for them when they only had one kid making you not quite as acceptable to them. Which is okay with you because they have been broken for the most part and can't determine or hear the difference between a loud cry, someone screaming bloody murder and a tiny whisper. Usually the multiple kids will deter you anyway because your baby gets all your attention and you don't understand the "neglect" they have or the lack of responsibility they have for their heathens for kids. You will find yourself doing many things in your family 3 pack during this time of life.

The whole point of this section is to take the changing of friends in stride. Your solid friends were there before, they always will be when you're in need. But if you're not in need, take the friend flow chart to make the correct friends for your stage of Daddyhood. You will see there is a Dad community out there that are at movies, in the parks, in play lands at restaurants and so much more.

TOPIC 31
ME NO SLEEPY

So many people think they become experts just because they have children. Skyler could have made several ladies pregnant and wouldn't consider himself any smarter than before it happened. Sure it may give us some life experiences, but if having sex and babies made you smart we would be a world even more sex crazy than we are now.

Skyler- And I have never heard of Nymphocation (a new kind of sex education). And don't go Google it, it doesn't exist...yet. Feel your situation out. I don't want my kids sleeping in my bed as much as the next person, however, I don't mind them sleeping in the same room. In fact in an emergency or when they are sick it actually puts my mind at ease. My solution was to put a little kid mattress off to the side of our bed. That way in the middle of the night when my son would wake up and come in he would go right to the little bed and lay down without having to wake us up to take him all the way back to his bed. Here was the key factor in that scenario. We would put him to sleep in his own bed. This would give me and my wife our alone time to hang out and do everything and nothing. So you can see that this is kind of a hybrid of those being stringent about no kids in the bedroom and those that let them sleep in the bed. Do what works for you. Just make sure you are getting your time with your lady and getting enough sleep to be a good dad. Remember, our culture we have the luxury of even having separate rooms for alone time.

Daniel- I was actually kicked out of the room for those first months when the doctors say the baby should be in the room because I snore too loudly. Well, I was able to stay with the first kid. She sleeps through anything. But the second still needs a sound machine to play ambient noise. So my snoring was definitely a problem and kept waking the baby. So out I went. Now that may not have been a good thing. My wife now felt completely alone not only all day while I was at work, but now also all night long. At this point, my Dude to Dad transition was far enough along that I took the baby monitor and set it up so that even though I was downstairs on the couches, I heard the baby and would go up and help as needed. Yeah, Dad points through the roof there.

THE WRAP UP

No, we aren't talking about condoms, we're talking about the end of this book. The good thing is it is just the beginning.

Skyler's Afterward: 2 Suspension Cables Down

I wasn't going to put this chapter in this book, after all, it is a book about guiding you through and too Daddyhood, not permanently taking away your ability. But after being constantly asked about this procedure and when is a good time to do it or how it is done I thought I would share my thoughts.

This procedure is done fairly quick and you are in and out of the office within several hours. The other good news is that most insurance will cover it as a specialist office visit which makes it really affordable. That is about where the good news ends. Other than the fact that if it is a successful surgery you will no longer have to fear the wrath of a woman peeing on a stick to see your fate.

I'm not going to tell you when getting a vasectomy is your best option, that is completely up to you when you are 100% sure you are done having kids. The operation can be reversed but I am telling you now that would be like someone throwing a fishing line into your nuts and hoping to snag the line in your tubes to pull out the parts and tie and sear them off to be reconnected for a POTENTIAL chance of success. Another words, be certain that you are done having kids.

On to the fun part, or at least you can have fun at my expense through the process. I thought I would be prepared when I went into the meeting so I shaved myself in the area that would need to be shaved anyway for the surgery. Come to find out, I didn't know and shaved the wrong area. So really it just looked like I had some irregular hair pattern or a flare of kinkiness. Neither were great options in my mind. Anyway, my wife and I show up at the appointment (yes my wife came, she wanted to see me go through just a glimmer of indecency and pain like she did birthing our children) and get escorted into a back room. My hands are sweaty at this point and I can feel my boys starting to retreat as far into my stomach as possible with the anticipation of the literature I read that was about to take place. The doctor comes in and double checks you are certain you want to go through with the process. Don't worry they are asking you, not checking their confidence. We proceed back to the operating office. This is probably the most uncomfortable part of the whole process. You get undressed from the waist down, throw your legs in some stirrups and let your junk dangle in the stale office breeze. The doctor comes in and gives you a nice ball bath. Much like washing your golf balls at the tee box before driving off the tee. Great. All clean and ready to go. Here are the words that made my eyes just about pop out of my head. The doctor said they would give me a shot that would numb it. How long do most doctors tell you before the shot takes affect and numbs the area. 2 to 3 seconds right? Or let's say 5 to be safe. No. The doctor says it stings for 30 mother f*#$ing seconds. 30. What is this some kind of joke or bondage session. What kind of shot hurts for 30 seconds. Come to find out, this one does, and this one did. Sure enough it was like a coiling snake that just spit venom in my tubes and I could feel it squirming through my body stinging its way. Beads of sweat just dripped off my forehead. Awe, finally its numb, it shouldn't hurt anymore. This is true, as it doesn't hurt. But let me ask you another question. Have you ever been kicked in the nuts before? That feeling where your stomach drops and you feel like you just might throw up one of your nuts? Well that came next. The little incision no biggie, but the pull of the tube and its pressure just doesn't feel right. They snag the tube, cut out a section, tie back the ends of both sides and burn it off. Yep, you actually get to smell burning with full realization of what's burning. Then a quick stitch back up and you're done. Other than the fact that you have two testicles and the process must be repeated on the other side. 30 more seconds! All in all you get out of their feeling pretty decent and you go home and ice yourself with some peas and tight underwear. Last word on this topic, get up slowly the next morning as you get up to go pee another drop kick feeling is about to occur and it almost makes you puke. Sex is the same. Your man juice is the same only down the fighters which is exactly what you wanted. The first few times is definitely trial and error. Just stay in tighty whiteys for a bit and the pinch will slowly fade and so will the memories of the day. Best quote I heard from this feeling is; "it feels like you are down a set of suspension cables at first."

ABOUT THE AUTHORS

Skyler has captivated his reading audience from the young age of 5 writing one-of-a-kind poetic verses. He has continued to expand his viewership through various social networks writing thought provoking, inspiring, humorous and engaging articles. Skyler has authored the books InCorporate Poetry and SkyWolfJones Poetry The Man Behind the Pen. He continues to write from his heart and his passions and it shows in his creative storytelling and masterful takes on life. His motto is "it's all good" and he considers himself first and foremost a family man. When Skyler is not writing he is playing sports, exploring in the mountains and going on family adventures. He has 3 incredible boys that include a red-head and twins and a beautiful wife who has earned wife of the year each consecutive year they've been married!

Daniel is a writer and publisher of fiction, poetry, and non-fiction. His first novel was published in 2009 and he has many more on the way. He's been creating stories since he was little and is currently working on his MFA in Writing Popular Fiction through Seton Hill University. When not working on From Dude to Dad with Skyler, he writes Mystery, Horror, SciFi, Fantasy, and Young Adult. He's a father of two beautiful girls and husband to a gorgeous wife and lives in Utah.

CPSIA information can be obtained
at www.ICGtesting.com
Printed in the USA
LVOW04s1830260416
485405LV00019B/710/P